STEP·BY·STEP
SUSHI

STEP·BY·STEP
SUSHI

KATSUJI YAMAMOTO
AND ROGER W HICKS

Quantum
Books

A QUANTUM BOOK

Published by
Quantum Publishing Ltd.
6 Blundell Street
London N7 9BH

ISBN 1-86160-450-5

QUMSUS

Printed in Singapore by
Star Standard Industries Pte Ltd.

CONTENTS

The Japanese have a genius for doing things beautifully. They also have a reputation for making things complicated. Who, for example, has not heard of the Japanese tea ceremony, which elevates a simple enough beverage into an art form?

Sushi can be almost as complicated as the tea ceremony, if you want to go into all the history and learn all the Japanese terms; and certainly, to become a master sushi chef (*itamae*) takes many years. On the other hand, you can learn enough about sushi to make it yourself at home surprisingly quickly. Many Japanese housewives do it all the time – although, of course, they apologize profusely for the fact that it is home-made.

INTRODUCTION

This is mainly a book about making your own sushi, but in order to appreciate sushi at home, you also need to know how to appreciate it when you eat out. There are all kinds of customs that are not immediately obvious: at the most basic, some people eat sushi 'set plates' for years before realizing that an *à la carte* order consists of two pieces, not one; or again, that if you are ordering *à la carte*, you do not order all the sushi you want at once. Instead, you order a few pieces, then a few more, and the meal is over when the *itamae* asks you if you want any more, and you say no. By watching the *itamae* you can also learn a great deal about making sushi at home!

It is also worth knowing a little about the history of sushi. One version says the rice was originally used to preserve fish, and was thrown away before the fish was eaten. Some people, however, acquired a taste for this rice, and that was the origin of sushi. Certainly, fermented fish dishes exist in many parts of Asia, including Japan: this is *nare-zushi* ('sushi' becomes *'zushi'* when it is hyphenated like this).

Another version, first recorded 1,200 years ago, says the emperor Keiko was once served raw clams with vinegar and liked the taste so much he made the inventor his head chef.

Whatever the truth, there is no doubt sushi is enormously popular, and becoming more popular all the time. Even people who are squeamish about raw fish can become enthusiastic converts, once they realize that sushi rivals the finest fillet steak (*filet mignon*) in texture, and the flavour is exquisite. And, even if they do not want to try the more exotic varieties, such as octopus or sea-urchin, they can stick with tuna or yellowtail, vegetarian sushi of various kinds and even a 'kosher' roll made with smoked salmon and cream cheese.

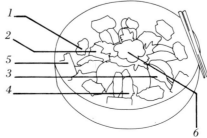

1 Ark shell (page 52);
2 tuna (page 92);
3 prawn (shrimp, page 80);
4 mackerel (page 62);
5 Egg Pancake (page 54);
6 Spicy Tuna Roll (page 84).

NIGIRI-ZUSHI
AND
MAKI

The type of sushi that is best known in the West, and indeed which is most popular in Japan, is called *nigiri-zushi* or finger sushi. It first became popular about 200 years ago as a fast food – but what an improvement over Western fast food!

Nigiri-zushi is what most people mean when they say 'sushi', and in many ways it is the simplest form, at least in concept. The chef carves a piece of raw fish (or any one of a number of other ingredients), puts a smear of *wasabi* (Japanese horseradish or Japanese mustard) on the bottom and places it on a little finger-shaped patty of vinegared sushi rice. Sometimes, there will be a 'strap' of *nori* (seaweed paper) around it as well. The whole thing is just solid enough to stay together in the fingers or when picked up with chopsticks, but it seems to melt when it is placed in your mouth. Needless to say, this is not quite as easy to prepare as it looks, but it is still something you can learn to do quite satisfactorily at home.

If the topping is soft or semi-liquid, as with some kinds of roe or sea urchin, the sushi-chef will build a little 'wall' of *nori* all the way around; such sushi are known as *gunkan-maki* or 'battleship sushi' from their resemblance to a man-of-war or battleship.

The next most usual kind of sushi is probably rolled sushi (*maki-zushi*). There are countless varieties of these, and sushi-chefs often have specialities which they have developed themselves. At the simplest, though, they consist of a sheet of *nori*, spread with sushi rice. In the centre, the chef puts fish, avocado, cucumber or anything else suitable, then rolls the whole thing up in a tight roll with the help of a flexible bamboo mat. The roll is then sliced which in the more expensive restaurants are arranged very artistically.

The most spectacular kinds of rolled sushi may have an additional layer of rice outside the *nori*, with fish and sometimes avocado rolled on the outside of this. This is where chefs like to show their vituosity!

A more casual variety of *maki-zushi* is the hand-rolled *maki*, which usually looks like an old-fashioned ice-cream cone rolled from *nori* and filled with sushi rice, and whatever takes the fancy of the customer or the sushi-chef. Strictly, any *maki* which is not pressed with the bamboo mat is *temaki*.

With any form of rolled sushi, a single roll, which may be cut into anything up to eight pieces constitutes an order *à la carte*.

Finally, there are various other kinds of finger sushi such as *inari* (stuffed fried tofu), Tiger Eye (stuffed squid, page 90) and cooked sushi.

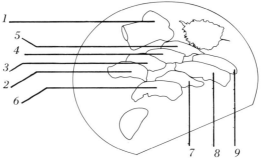

1 *Tuna* maki *(page 84)*;
2 *yellowtail (page 92)*;
3 *tuna (page 92)*;
4 *cooked squid (page 86)*;
5 *prawn (shrimp; page 80)*;
6 *octopus (page 64)*;
7 *mackerel (page 62)*;
8 *Egg Pancake (page 54)*;
9 *sea eel (page 76)*.

Hako-zushi *(box sushi)* is
made using a special
pressing box with a
removable top and base.

OTHER TYPES OF SUSHI AND SASHIMI

Scattered Sushi *(Chirashi-zushi)*

As you might expect, the way in which the ingredients are 'scattered' in *chirashi-zushi* is rarely careless. This is, however, the very simplest type of sushi to make, if you are not too worried about the aesthetics.

Almost anything can be used in *chirashi-zushi*. As well as fish, you can use vegetables, omelette, chicken, scrambled egg and *shiitake* mushrooms. There is more about this form of sushi on page 72.

Steamed Sushi *(Mushi-zushi)*

If you make *chirashi-zushi* with raw, soaked rice (see instructions for soaking, page 42), and then steam it in a bowl for 15 minutes, you have *mushi-zushi*. This is one of the few types of sushi which can be re-heated as 'leftovers' – though it still won't keep for more than a day or two in the refrigerator.

Box Sushi *(Hako-zushi)*

Hako-zushi requires a pressing-box, as illustrated. It may be made with one or more kinds of fish, but differs from *nigiri-zushi* in that the rice and fish are pressed into one big block, which is then sliced up for serving.

Fermented Sushi *(Nare-zushi)*

Nare-zushi has already been mentioned as one of the possible origins of sushi. Although it is still made in some districts of Japan, it is something of an acquired taste, and is not conveniently, or safely, made at home. Some types of fermented sushi take a year to reach the right stage of aging.

Sashimi

Sashimi is effectively sushi without the rice. The fish may be raw or cooked, marinated or unmarinated. Some types can take a little getting used to: whole baby squid taste delicious, but they look somewhat unnerving to a Western eye.

Sashimi is sometimes eaten as a prelude to sushi, sometimes as an appetizer to a cooked meal and sometimes in its own right.

An itamae's-*eye view of a*
sushi bar: a never-ending
blur of work.

Many restaurants serve sushi, and this is a book about making it at home; but the true *tsu* (sushi connoisseur) will haunt sushi bars.

The story is that sushi bars were originally stand-up bars where people stopped for a quick snack on the way from one place to another, before going home after work, or even between acts at the theatre. Because they were snack bars, no alcohol was served and the whole emphasis was on speed.

Since those days, sushi bars have grown very much more elaborate. The most expensive can rival a fine French restaurant in price, while at the other extreme there are still places where a television stands over the bar and the patrons are mostly working men. There are even mechanized sushi bars, where the *itamae* works surrounded by an oval conveyor belt, and the plates are carried slowly past the customers as they sit around the outside. The plates are colour coded, and the reckoning is conducted on the number of plates and the colours of their borders; the *itamae* simply replaces whatever is running low.

A classic sushi bar sells only sushi, and has only a sushi bar – no tables. Outside Japan, such places are rare. Even so, unless a place has a bar, the *tsu* or would-be *tsu* will not eat there, and sitting at the bar is the best way to eat sushi.

You will be given *wasabi*, a green paste known either as Japanese horseradish (because it is made from a root) or Japanese mustard (because it is *hot*) and *gari* (pickled ginger slices). *Gari* is also known as *sudori shōga*, but the true sushi lover will always use the shorter word. You may or may not get a hot towel to clean your hands; traditionally, running water was available so you could wash them. If you don't get tea automatically, ask for it. If you want to drink anything else, order that as well (see overleaf).

Many sushi bars have printed lists of sushi, on which you, your waitress, or the *itamae* himself check off the things you want. Alternatively, an old-fashioned *itamae* will keep all the reckoning (including orders) in his head. There is no particular order for eating them; just order what you like. If you ask the *itamae* what is best, he will usually tell you: he is more interested in his reputation than in palming off inferior fish.

Eat the sushi either with chopsticks or with your fingers. Eat a little ginger, and sip some tea between pieces of sushi to clear your palate. Drink *sake before* a mouthful, not after.

SUSHI BARS

TEA

The only thing a purist will drink with sushi is tea – Japanese green tea, of course, not Indian or China tea, and always on its own without any sweetening or other additives.

Japanese tea comes in many grades, and the cheapest *bancha* grade is perfectly acceptable with sushi. While some people serve higher-grade *sencha* tea, the very best *hikicha* and *gyokuro* teas are not normally served with sushi as their delicacy would be overwhelmed by the taste of the fish.

The one thing all Japanese teas have in common is that they are made with water that is *not* boiling. As a general rule, the more expensive the tea, the shorter the infusion time and the lower the temperature: 1–2 minutes at about 150°F/65°C for *gyokuro*, 2 minutes at about 170°F/75–80°C for *sencha*, and 2–3 minutes at anything less than boiling for *bancha*. *Bancha* leaves are sometimes re-used to make a second infusion.

If the tea is made with leaves, they should neither float, which indicates insufficient steeping, nor sink, which indicates excessive steeping. In a perfect cup of tea, the leaves should float in the middle of the cup; if they stand vertically, it is regarded as a very good omen.

In sushi bars, the tea may be made from powdered leaves, as the infusion is quicker to prepare this way. It should always be served in big *yunomi* beakers, which are refilled on a 'bottomless pot' principle so you always have tea to accompany your sushi. As you sit down, the *itamae*, or one of his assistants, should bring tea automatically; if this does not happen, just ask.

1 Warm the teapot and put 1 heaped teaspoon of leaves per person into the pot.

2 Pour boiled water which has been allowed to cool a little over the tea leaves. Cover the pot and allow to steep for 1–2 minutes.

3 Warm the teacups and, holding down the lid of the teapot, fill the teacups two-thirds full.

4 To drink the tea, pick up the cup with your right hand and support it on your left. It is customary to make a slight slurping noise when drinking tea, particularly if it is hot.

DRINKS WITH SUSHI

The etiquette of sake-*drinking requires that you fill your neighbour's cup but never your own. In Japan a* sake *cup is never allowed to remain empty for long. The cup may be filled to the brim. Sake should, in theory, be downed in one. The toast is* 'Kampai!'.

Although the only traditional drink with sushi is tea, the Japanese are remarkably flexible about what they drink with it, and even those who drink tea with their sushi will often enjoy an alcoholic drink beforehand.

The usual choices are normally either *sake* or beer. A purist, assuming he or she does not drink tea, will go for dry *sake*, but as the advertisements in the sushi bars show, Japanese brewers are out to change this: Sapporo, Kirin and Asahi all vie for customers, with illustrated guides to sushi beside their beer menus.

As an alternative to *sake* or beer, some Japanese drink whisky. Scotch is the most highly regarded, but Japanese whisky is no longer a joke: one of the finest brands is Suntory, which can stand comparison with any good blended Scotch. Drinking wine with sushi is more unusual.

If you are buying *sake* to drink at home, use *kara kuchi*, the dry kind, and remember that the grades – Special, First and Second – refer to the strength rather than the flavour. *Sake* is 16–19% alcohol. *Mirin* is cooking *sake*, not for drinking.

Sake is sometimes served iced, but is more usually served warm or hot. To heat it, pour it into *sake* bottles and lower them into almost boiling water. Alternatively, for a short cut, use a microwave oven! The correct serving temperature is blood heat or above, 98–105°F/36–40°C

Japanese beers are readily available in many places; otherwise, German beers or even Irish stout like Guinness are very good.

Whisky goes frighteningly easily with sushi, especially the stronger flavoured kinds. Be warned – four friends can easily dispose of a bottle without really noticing!

If you want to drink wine, try a fortified wine, such as dry sherry, or a white wine. Red wines rarely go with sushi, though rose wines are all right if you like them.

Sake *is served in small*
flasks and drunk from very
small ceramic cups. Always
raise your cup to receive
sake, *supporting the cup on*
your left hand and holding
it with your right.

SUSHI AND HEALTH

The praises of seafood have long been sung by the health establishment, but few diet books address the specific question of sushi.

First, raw fish contains many nutrients, including trace minerals and vitamins that are partially or completely destroyed by cooking.

Second, sushi is tailor-made for those who are concerned about cholesterol. The only major exception is *tamago* (egg roll), and you would be hard put to eat enough of this for it to matter.

Third, sushi is very low in calories. It is impossible to give a per-piece caloric rating, partly because of variations in ingredients and partly because the individual pieces in some restaurants are twice the size that you find in others, but each order of two pieces of sushi or one roll is likely to be under 100 calories, often well under.

Sushi rice is about 25–40 calories per 1oz/30g, and fish runs from about 20–80 calories per 1oz/30g. Only the fattiest tuna is likely to exceed the upper limit, while shellfish and non-oily fish are much closer to the lower limit. Other ingredients frequently used, such as *kornbot* or *nori* (seaweed), *gari* (pickled ginger) and *wasabi* (Japanese horseradish or mustard), are unlikely to be significantly fattening.

A good meal might consist of half a dozen orders; if you drank tea, with effectively zero calories, you might consume 500 calories. Gluttony, with a dozen orders and three bottles of *sake*, might push the penalty up to the 1,500 calorie mark.

Looking on the negative side, there are three things to consider: salt, parasites and *fugu* (or *fougou*).

Raw fish is fairly salty to start with, and soy sauce adds still more sodium to the meal. In most cases, however, there is still very little salt to worry about, and if you are preparing sushi at home, you can reduce the salt or use a salt substitute.

Parasites are found in various types of fish, especially salmon (which is why salmon is not eaten in Japan) but freezing is said to kill them and (more importantly) also their eggs.

The famous *fugu*, or blow-fish, contains a deadly toxin in the liver and ovaries, and every year in Japan about 200 people die in agony (though usually very quickly) from eating improperly prepared *fugu*, which by law is only prepared by government-licensed *itamae*. The risks are very small, but if you have any doubts, simply do not order this very expensive dish, which is rarely available outside Japan anyway.

Yellowtail (page 92/93), a member of the jack fish family, similar to tuna, from Pacific waters, is one of the fattiest fish, but this serving probably represents 80–90 calories. Also, because you order one type of sushi at a time, you have time to appreciate the food – and to ask yourself if you really need that 10th order!

SUSHI
AT
HOME

The rest of this book is concerned principally with preparing sushi at home. Before going on to details, there are a number of general points worth making.

To begin with, not all sushi is raw. Even where the fish is sometimes served raw, like squid, there are often older ways of preparation in which it is cooked, and many *tsu* prefer these.

With some types of shellfish, especially prawns (shrimp), only the very freshest specimens are served raw: the 'dancing shrimp', still quivering with life after it has been killed and prepared, is the classic example. Less fresh examples are cooked.

A surprising amount of sushi eaten today has been frozen. Even prawns (shrimp) served raw may have been frozen – though it would have been quick-frozen very carefully, and it will not be cheap.

Many types of fish, especially shellfish, for sushi are easily available *only* pre-packaged and frozen, unless you go to the most expensive sushi bars in Japan. With pre-packaged toppings, fish preparation amounts only to long, slow thawing (left overnight in the refrigerator).

Substitutions and local variations are commonplace. Salmon, for example, is a common fish for sushi in California; in Japan it is hardly used at all. For this reason, it is not given a separate heading to itself in this book, but is covered on the same page as halibut. Where practicable, other fish which are treated in the same way are grouped together on the same pages.

Because of the increasing popularity of sushi, fish is now air-freighted around the world on a regular basis; the Japanese, in particular, buy from all over the world. On the other hand, many sushi bars in Tokyo are now out of the reach of the common man because they are so very expensive.

Not all forms of sushi are expensive, however. The moulded 'imitation crab', made from shaped and seasoned white fish, makes an excellent low-cost sushi topping. Even so, it is generally easier for the person who is making sushi at home to serve a relatively restricted range of fish, perhaps as an appetizer rather than as the main meal. It is not practicable to try to emulate a sushi bar, which may have a couple of dozen varieties of fish, at home.

Where recipes for cooked food are given in this book, pay more attention to the order in which things are done, and to the timing, than to precise quantities. In particular, quantities of sugar, salt and soy sauce may be adjusted over a wide range to suit individual tastes.

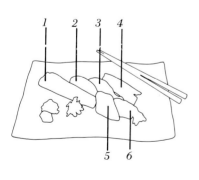

Easy sushi to make at home: 1 vegetable temaki *(page 88); 2 prawn (shrimp; page 80); 3 yellowtail (page 92); 4 imitation crab meat; 5 gunkan-maki; 6 wilted* daikon *sprouts.*

IN THE KITCHEN

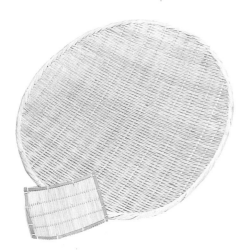

The most important thing is a plentiful supply of running water, because you are going to be washing your hands, your knives, your cloths and your rolling mat very frequently. A lever-operated tap (faucet) is much more convenient than an old-fashioned one.

The *manaita* (chopping board) can be of any material: wood is traditional, but plastic works just as well. About 12×18 in /30×45 cm is adequate. Because it is hard to remove the smell of fish from a wooden board, reserve one board (or one side of a board) exclusively for cutting fish and shellfish.

A master sushi chef will have a number of knives *(hōchō)*. Most of the work is done with three: the all-purpose *banno-bōchō*, the cleaverlike *deba-bōchō*, and the square-tipped *nakiri-bōchō* for cutting vegetables. There are, however, many others. Two of the most important, owned by many sushi chefs, are the long, thin *sashimi-bōchō* for slicing boned fillets and the *sushikiri-bōchō* (commonly called *yanagi*).

In practice, a long, fairly light kitchen knife of high quality can be used for most purposes: choose the size (typically a 7–10 in/17.5–25cm blade) that suits you best. Keep the blade razor-sharp; making sushi with blunt knives tears the fish, gives ragged cuts, and is generally unsatisfactory. After use, wash and dry the knife and put it away carefully.

A *zaru* (strainer) is essential for draining water off foods. A plastic or enamel colander will do, but a proper bamboo *zaru* is not expensive. It must be dried and aired completely after use, or it will quickly become musty and mouldy.

A *makisu* (rolling mat), an omelette pan, a grater, a fish-scaler and thin, round skewers complete the *batterie de cuisine*. A traditional Japanese omelette pan *(tamago-yaki nabe)* is square and about ¾ in/2 cm deep; the shape makes it easier to fold the omelette repeatedly and to cut it into neat strips. Cast-iron pans are traditional, though many cooks use heavy aluminium. If you want to make box sushi, as described on pages 10 and 11, you will also need a sushi-box.

Kitchen tools for preparing rice are described on pages 42 and 43.

A *zaru (bamboo strainer) is the traditional utensil for straining food.*

The oroshi-gane *(Japanese grater) is extremely fine-toothed, made of metal or ceramic, and often has a sill to collect the draining juices. It is ideal for grating daikon, ginger and wasabi, although the finest tooth of a Western grater will do.*

A *small flexible makisu (bamboo mat) is used for making sushi. Sushi may be rolled by hand, but will be less firmly and evenly packed.*

An itamae *takes his knives very seriously: some sets are handed down from father to son. They are supplied with wooden sheaths, as shown.*

SUSHI TECHNIQUES

In this book, we have consciously restricted ourselves to presenting sushi which could be made at home. Up to a certain point, sushi is a matter of technique. Beyond that point, it is pure art. What you are paying for in the very best sushi restaurants in Tokyo is not the ingredients, or even the *ambiance* of the restaurant; it is the grace and skill with which the ingredients are arranged.

While this sort of a presentation adds greatly to the experience of eating in a great sushi restaurant, it is easy to be intimidated by such artistry. Instead, build on the basic techniques taught here. Watch the *itamae* at work when you eat out, and, in time, you can start to worry about art as well as technique.

Above all else, the secret of sushi-making is to keep your hands wet. Otherwise, the fish will dry out and the rice will stick to your fingers. This was a recurrent problem throughout the photography for this book: an *itamae* normally works fast, and slowing down means dried-out sushi. Add about 2tbsp/30ml/1fl oz vinegar to 2 cups/500ml/16fl oz water in a bowl, and float a slice of lemon in it. Wet your hands and your knife with this.

Knives are used wet, and cleaned frequently. Either wipe the blade with a damp cloth, or dip the tip in water and tap the handle on the counter, holding the knife upright, to spread the water. Take great care not to transfer flavours, especially onion, to other ingredients with the knife.

Trim all fish mercilessly, both for aesthetics and for the palate; shreds of skin, bones and discoloured parts have no place in sushi. With fatty fish, trim off the very dark meat by the belly, as this is too strongly flavoured for most people.

Sushi chefs use a pair of heavy flat-ended tweezers to remove bones from filleted fish. Check visually and with the tips of your fingers.

When cutting fish from a squared-off fillet (the form in which it is often bought), slice the end piece as shown opposite, do not use it for *nigiri-zushi* because it will not be as tender as a piece cut on the bias, and it will not look right. This technique is known as *sakudori*. Awkward-shaped scraps can be used in rolls, where appearance is not important.

Long chopsticks for cooking are not essential, but they can be very useful. Wooden ones are used for beating the eggs for omelettes and for manipulating the omelette in the pan, while the sort with fine metal tips are useful for making the final adjustments to finished sushi.

Small pieces of sushi look less impressive than large pieces, are more work, and dry out faster; but they are easier to eat in a single mouthful.

Fish is always cut on the bias, like this.

The easiest way to divide a sheet of nori *is with a knife – don't attempt to break it by hand.*

Vegetables are often diced from short lengths; this is much easier than trying to dice a long, tapering vegetable.

Keep a bowl of water with a slice of lemon to hand for wetting the knife.

BUYING FISH

*hoice of the finest and
eshest ingredients is
bsolutely fundamental to
apanese cooking, and fish
arkets are visited on a
uily basis by restaurant
nd home chefs alike.*

For sushi, absolute freshness is of the utmost import-ance. Ideally, the fish should be fresh-caught; some sushi restaurants in Japan will even cut slices from *live* fish, returning them to the tank afterwards. If the fish are frozen immediately after they have been caught, some types of fatty fish and shellfish can be thawed and used for sushi; other types of fish will become too watery or discoloured.

In the West, if you cannot buy the fish from the pier, you should go to a fishmonger you can trust. Look for bright, clear eyes with no sunkenness or blood, intact, glossy scales, bright red gills and flesh which is resilient and springs back when you poke it. Above all, there should be no 'fishy' smell; at most, a slight hint of the sea. Once you have bought the fish, it should be dressed (see overleaf) as soon as possible, then the dressed fish should be either consumed immediately or refrigerated. For short spells in the refrigerator, such as a few hours, covering with a damp cloth is best; overnight, use cling film (plastic wrap).

If you catch the fish yourself, make an incision behind the gills, and another just in front of the tail, and bleed it immediately: it can then be kept on ice in first-class condition. If it thrashes around, dies slowly and is not bled, it will be of very inferior quality.

If you are buying frozen fish, let it thaw as slowly as possible, preferably overnight in the refrigerator. Soak-ing in water can entail a serious loss of flavour, but if you are in a hurry, add 2tsp/10ml/2tsp salt per 2 cups/500ml/16fl oz water for freshwater fish and 1tbsp/15ml/½oz salt per 2 cups/500ml/16fl oz water for saltwater fish.

If you are buying fillets or cuts, rather than whole fish, be sure that the meat is firm, it has a sheen when it is cut and the blood is bright red.

Shellfish should be alive when bought. This applies equally to all varieties, though live squid and octopus are harder to come by than live clams or abalone, or even prawns (shrimp). Live shellfish will not float, it feels heavy when picked up and remains firmly closed. They will live for some time – even days – in water in a refrigerator that is not too cold (35–40°F/5–6°C is fine).

FILLETING FISH

There are two ways to fillet a fish for sushi. The first, used for most fish except flatfish, *sanmai oroshi* gives three fillets and a skeleton. The second *gomai oroshi* is used for flatfish and for larger fish, and is described in detail overleaf.

Three-piece Fillet
(Sanmai Oroshi)

If the fish requires scaling (this one does not, it is served with the skin on), hold the head of the fish firmly and scrape off the scales – be careful as you will be cutting towards yourself. Clean both sides. Alternatively, hold the tail. Do not hold the body, as this will bruise the flesh and destroy its firmness. Throughout the process, wash frequently in lightly salted water.

1 Place the fish with the head facing to the left (if right-handed). With a sharp knife, make a diagonal cut at the base of the head to remove it.

2 Slice backwards along the belly towards the anal (pelvic) fin.

3 Remove the stomach and viscera.

5 Taking the piece of fish containing the backbone, rest the left hand gently on the fish and slide the knife along the back between the flesh and bone from the head to the tail.

4 Rest the left hand lightly on top of the fish and cut along the back from head to the tail so that the knife skims the rib cage. Lift off the fillet.

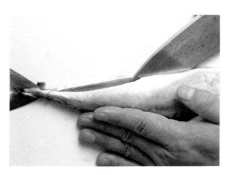

6 Reverse the fish and cut through the base of the tail, releasing the second fillet. Pluck out any bones remaining in the fillets.

7 The fish is now in three pieces: a left and a right fillet, and a skeleton. If the fillets are very large, cut them in half lengthways – or, of course, use the *gomai oroshi* described overleaf.

FILLETING FISH

Five-piece Fillet *(Gomai Oroshi)*

There are two variations of five-piece filleting technique. One is used for flatfish, and the other for large fish such as bonita, a member of the tuna family. If you try to bone large fish *sanmai oroshi*, you run the risk of damaging the flesh by trying to remove too large a fillet at once. Bruised fish with 'shakes' in the flesh is no good for sushi.

VARIATION 1: FLATFISH

1 Resting the left hand (if you are right handed) on the head of the fish, make two deep cuts behind the gills.

2 Turn the fish and remove the head. Squeeze out the stomach and viscera and clean the fish thoroughly under cold running water.

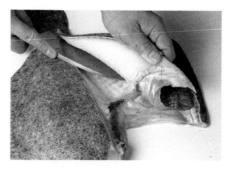

3 Turn the fish again, and cut down to the spine from head to tail.

4 Keeping the knife blade flat, slide it along the bone to release the flesh.

With a large fish like tuna or, as here, bonita, you first gut the fish and remove the head, then proceed as in the following steps:

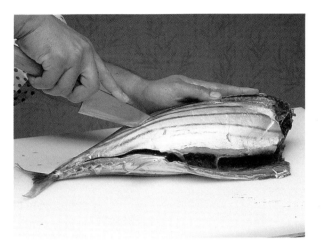

5 Starting from the tail, slide the knife along the outside edge of the fish to release the first fillet. Reverse the fish and follow steps 3 to 5 to remove the second fillet from the top of the fish.

1 Make a long cut along the lateral line from head to tail.

6 Turn the fish over and again remove a left and a right fillet.

2 Make a second incision, coming down from the spine. Remove the fillet.

7 The result is a fish in five pieces, as shown. You will also have four pieces of *engawa*, the meat next to the side fins. *Engawa* is much prized, but only a large fish will provide enough to be worth using.

3 Remove the belly fillet by cutting from above. Repeat steps 1 to 3 for the other side.

VEGETABLES

Daikon and other vegetables are sometimes peeled in a long continuous sheet. The sheet is then cut into 8 in/20 cm lengths, stacked and finely sliced to make an edible 'angel hair' garnish.

Pickled daikon (radish), cucumber, avocado, wakegi (spring onion/scallion) and root ginger.

Avocado: Using avocados in sushi is a comparatively recent innovation. Predictably, they are especially popular in California, one of the world's leading producers. Avocado is delicious in *maki* (rolls) of various kinds, and is also used to add colour to a Rainbow Roll (page 66).

Carrots (ninjin): As with avocados, carrots are used both for their culinary value and for their colour. They are a prime ingredient in Vegetable Rolls (page 50).

Cucumber (kappa): Cucumbers are a classic ingredient in Vegetable Rolls, and are also widely used as a garnish (see pages 40 and 41). Japanese cucumbers are smaller and less watery than the larger British and American varieties.

Daikon: Sometimes called a 'radish', this is much bigger and milder than the small red radish familiar to most westerners. If you cannot find it anywhere else, try Indian and Pakistani shops: the name in Hindi is *mooli*.

Kampyō: Dried gourd; see pages 38 and 39.

Nattō: A kind of glutinous soya bean preparation, not readily available (or widely liked) in the West.

Onion (wakegi): Spring onions (green onions, scallions) are sometimes used in the more modern forms of sushi. A Kosher Roll (page 82), for example, contains smoked salmon, cream cheese and spring onions. Generally, though, onion overwhelms the delicate taste of sushi.

Seaweed: In sushi, the most usual seaweed is the dark green or black *nori*. It is effectively a kind of paper made from chopped, dried purple laver, and is used to wrap sushi. It rapidly loses its aroma unless it is frozen, in which case it is good for two or three months or more. Before use, lightly toast one side of the sheet of *nori* to bring out the flavour; about 30 seconds over a gas flame is ideal. Toasting both sides seems to diminish the taste again. A full sheet of *nori* is 7×8¼in/17.5×21cm.

Ao nori is a flaked version of the same thing, used as a seasoning.

Kombu is used to make *dashi* soup stock (pages 36 and 37).

Shiitake mushrooms are sometimes used in sushi (pages 38 and 39).

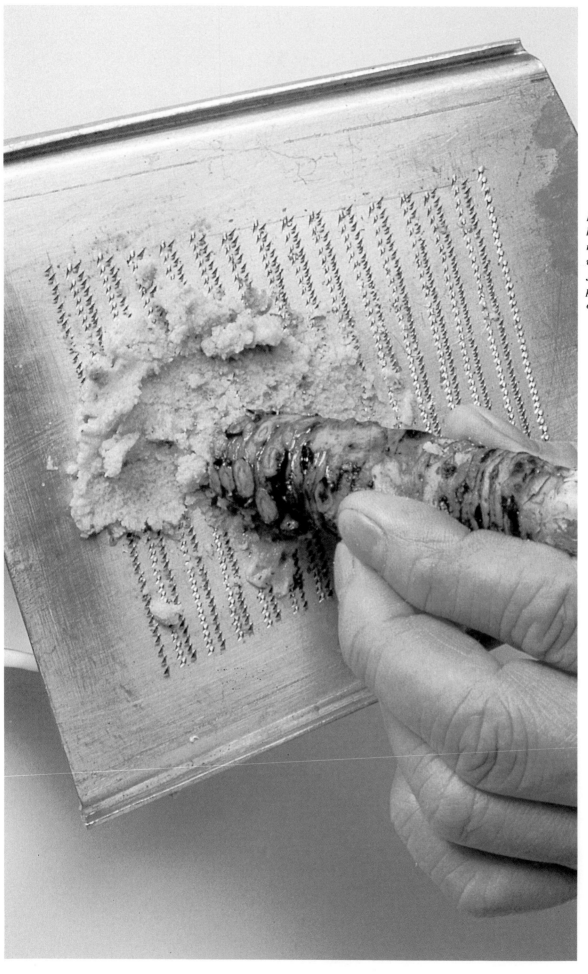

Fresh wasabi *(Japanese horseradish or Japanese mustard) like this, left, is very hard to obtain outside Japan. Prepared* wasabi *or powdered* wasabi *are the alternatives.*

OTHER
INGREDIENTS

Dark soy sauce is used for general cooking purposes, while the lighter variety (on the right) is used where colouring is not required.

Japanese su (rice vinegar) should always be used when available, but diluted cider vinegar may be substituted.

Mirin (sweetened cooking sake) can be bought ready-made in bottles.

Bean curd (tōfu): Basic tofu no longer needs special introduction: the creamy-white cubes are a familiar sight in many Western supermarkets and health food shops. The kind of tofu used in *Inari* (pages 60 and 61) is, however deep fried.

Some people use tofu instead of rice under *nigiri-zushi*; it is very good for you, but rather bland. Well-flavoured fish and spicy condiments are advisable.

Cream cheese: A very un-Japanese ingredient (the Japanese share the usual Oriental view of 'rotten milk') which is nevertheless making more and more appearances in various kinds of *maki*.

Eggs: Chicken eggs are used to make *Tamago* omelettes (page 54), and quail eggs are used as a garnish, for example with roe. A *Sake* Shooter is a quail egg yolk in the bottom of a glass of *sake*.

Katsuo-bushi: Dried bonito flakes used to make *dashi* soup stock (pages 36 and 37).

Mirin: Also known as 'sweet *sake*', this is used for a number of purposes, including cooking sushi rice. If you cannot get *mirin*, dissolve heaped ½ cup/120g/4oz sugar in ½-1 cup/120-250ml/4-8 fl oz hot dry *sake*.

Miso: Fermented soya bean paste. The lighter varieties tend to be less salty and sweeter than the darker varieties.

Pickled plums (ume-boshi): Sometimes used in vegetarian *maki*.

Rice vinegar (su): Japanese rice vinegar is pale straw in colour and very mild; do not confuse it with red or black rice vinegar, which are strongly flavoured. Wine, cider and malt vinegars are too strong for most Japanese dishes – diluted cider vinegar can be used, though.

Soy sauce (shōyu): Japanese or American soy sauces are more delicate than Chinese. Regular dark soy sauce (*koi kuchi shōyu*) is normally used; if you are on a low-sodium diet, use the sodium-reduced variety, but do not confuse it with *usui kuchi shōyu* which is lighter in colour but higher in salt content than *koi kuchi shōyu*.

Sugar: Even those who love Japanese food are sometimes shocked to discover how much sugar it contains. In sushi, sugar is used in rice preparation and in making some kinds of glaze.

Sake is the national alcoholic drink of Japan and is the most suitable accompaniment to a Japanese meal, after authentic Japanese tea.

DASHI AND SOUP

Dashi is one of the fundamental ingredients of much Japanese cooking. It is encountered less with sushi than with other dishes, but it is still used in preparing several kinds of cooked ingredients and for soup.

Dashi

The ingredients are simple: *katsuo-bushi* (dried bonito flakes), *kombu* (seaweed) and water. Traditionally *katsuo-bushi* comes in a block like a mahogany plank and is shaved for use. Today, however, most people buy ready-made flakes. Check the expiry date because anything over six months old will be past its prime.

■ The proportions are also simple in dry measure, ½ cup/120g/1oz *katsuo-bushi* per 1 cup/250ml/8fl oz water, seasoned with 2-3sq in/5-7.5sq cm.

■ Put the *kombu* in a pot with the cold water, then bring to the boil. As soon as the water begins to boil remove the *kombu*. Leaving the *kombu* in makes the stock (broth) bitter and cloudy.

■ Add the *katsuo-bushi* to the stock and turn up the heat. Do not stir. As soon as the stock is boiling again, remove the pan from the heat. When the *katsuo-bushi* flakes sink, the *dashi* is ready. Strain the flakes out; leaving them in will make the *dashi* too fishy. Both the *kombu* and the *katsuo-bushi* can be re-used to make a less strongly flavoured *dashi*.

■ Vary the quantities of *katsuo-bushi* to suit your individual taste; at first, many Westerners use less. You may also care to mix *dashi* with chicken, beef or even vegetable stock.

Soups

Although there are many kinds of soup with a *dashi* base, the ones usually encountered with sushi are *suimono* and *miso-dashi*.

SUIMONO

To make *suimono*, heat *dashi* with a little *tōfu* (bean curd), fish or chicken. If you are using *tōfu*, do not allow the soup to boil or the *tōfu* will disintegrate. Add either a few flakes of seaweed or a chopped spring onion (scallion). In a classic *suimono*, there is also a seasonal garnish *(sui-kichi)* such as pepper leaves, but this is both perfectionist and unnecessarily difficult in the West.

MISO-DASHI

Miso-dashi is much the same thing, thickened with about 2tbsp/30g/1oz *miso* to 2 cups/500ml/16fl oz *dashi*. *Miso-dashi* may be made with *tōfu*, seasonal vegetables or seafood.

Kombu *comes as leathery, dried strips of seaweed. Although* katsuo boshi *is traditionally sold in a solid block which is shaved for use, most people now buy it ready-shaved.*

A beautifully garnished miso-dashi *made with* tōfu *and leeks.*

KAMPYŌ AND SHIITAKE

Kampyō is made from the dried skin of a Japanese gourd and is packaged in long strips. It is used in some kinds of *maki* (rolls) and in *chirashi-zushi* (scattered sushi), as well as in other recipes.

To reconstitute *kampyō*, wash a small amount in water with a scrubbing motion and rub with salt. Soak for at least a couple of hours, or overnight. To cook and season *kampyō* for use in sushi, boil it – about 10 minutes, until it is translucent, then simmer for about 5 minutes in *dashi* (page 36) seasoned with 1tbsp/15ml/½oz sugar, 1½tsp/7.5ml/ 1½tsp soy sauce, and a pinch of salt for each 1 cup/250ml/8fl oz *dashi*.

Shiitake mushrooms are normally sold dried. They smell quite strong and are very expensive but are essential for an authentic Japanese flavour in some dishes. In any case, most of the smell vanishes when they are soaked. They also gain considerably in weight after soaking; a small amount of dried *shiitake* will last a long time and go a long way.

If you are in a hurry, you can soak *shiitake* mushrooms for as little as 30–40 minutes, then remove the hard cores and stems before cooking. Soaking overnight – 24 hours is fine – allows you to use the whole mushroom and makes for greater tenderness.

To prepare seasoned *shiitake* mushrooms for serving use the following recipe:

INGREDIENTS

4–6 *shiitake* mushrooms, well soaked and squeezed dry
with ⅔ cup/150ml/5fl oz soaking liquid reserved

1 cup/250ml/8fl oz *dashi*

dash of sake – about 1tsp/5ml/1tsp

2tbsp/30ml/6tsp sugar

1tbsp/15ml/3tsp soy sauce

1tbsp/5ml/1tsp *mirin*

METHOD

■ Mix the mushroom liquid, the *dashi* and the *sake*. Bring to the boil in a heavy-based pan, then add the mushrooms. Reduce heat to a simmer and cook about 3 minutes, basting frequently.

■ Add the sugar and continue to simmer until the liquid has been reduced to half (this should take less than 10 minutes). Add the soy sauce and cook for another 3–4 minutes, then add the *mirin*. Continue cooking over a high heat, shaking the pan, until the mushrooms are evenly coated with glaze.

Kampyō, *before and after preparation*

Shiitake *mushrooms*

GARNISHES

The line between ingredients and garnishes can be hard to draw: after all, a sushi meal is an aesthetic whole.

Kappa (cucumber): Cutting vegetables for garnishes is an essential part of Japanese cuisine, and one of the most exquisite techniques involves the 'pine-tree' cut shown here.

1 Using the end of a cucumber, score parallel lines of equal length lengthwise.

2 Cut at right angles, with the knife parallel to the board.

3 Push the cut part to one side.

4 Repeat, pushing the cut parts alternately left and right.

5 Decorate with smelt roe for real colour.

*trips of gari (above) can be
lled up to create a 'rose'
r garnishing (right).*

*Take a slice of kamaboko
nd cut a slit along the
entre of the slice. To form a
lait', insert one end of the
ice through the slit and
ull under.*

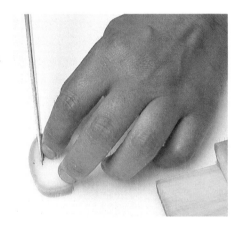

*To make a 'knot', take a
ice of kamaboko and cut a
it as above. Cut 2 oblong
ticks' from another slice of
amboko and tuck into the
it to create 'ends'.*

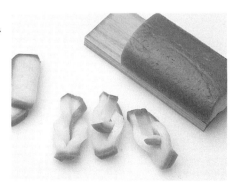

*A block of kamaboko, with
'plait' and two 'knot'
arnishes.*

Daikon: Cutting *daikon* into ornamental shapes is also a common practice; many of the techniques for *daikon* are also applicable to carrot, and some can also be used on cucumber.

The easiest way to produce the flower-shape is to use a small device like a biscuit (cookie) cutter, though a traditional-minded chef will carve cylinders 2in/5cm long and then slice them. Another technique involves shaving off a 'thick peel' as though you were using a pencil sharpener; the 'thick peel' can then be cut on the bias and will curl attractively.

Gari (pickled ginger): Known to sushi-lovers as *gari* rather than the conventional Japanese *shōga*, this pink pickled root ginger is eaten in small quantities between orders to clear the palate and increase the appreciation of the next order.

Goma (sesame seeds): These are used at the discretion of the *itamae* to enhance certain kinds of sushi. For the best flavour, they should be dry roasted or toasted in a hot cast-iron pan for about a minute before they are used; keep them moving to avoid popping and burning. *Shiro goma* and *muki goma* are respectively unhulled and hulled white sesame seeds.

Oba: The beefsteak plant gives this hearty-looking leaf, prized both for its appearance and its scent.

Hiyashi-wakame: A type of seaweed. It is sold dried but is soaked and shredded to give a slippery, bright-green garnish.

Kamaboko (fish cake): *Kamaboko* is frequently used as an edible garnish. You can make 'knots' or 'plaits (braids)' by cutting a slit in the middle of a strip of fish cake, and then either forcing the end of the strip through the slot to create a plait or making two more cuts (to create 'ends') and pushing them through the slit.

Wasabi: Sometimes called 'Japanese horseradish' because it is derived from a root, the name 'Japanese mustard' describes the taste better. Fresh root is extremely difficult to find, and very expensive, but dried powdered *wasabi* is readily available and affordable.

SUSHI RICE

Sushi rice is made from a matured short-grain rice
Some sushi chefs even have their rice merchants mix
rice of differing degrees of maturity to achieve the desired
result.

Rice is best cooked in about its own weight of water
very new rice, which contains more moisture, requires
less, and older rice may require more. Experiment to
get the best results. You will find it easier if you stick
with a single brand of rice, as the moisture content is
likely to be more constant.

- Wash the rice thoroughly until the water comes clear
  Let the washed rice dry and swell for an hour.
- To cook rice easily, you need a pot with a tight
  fitting lid. Bring the rice to the boil over a medium
  heat, then cover tightly. Boil over a high flame for 2
  minutes, then a medium flame for 5 minutes, and a
  low flame for about 15 minutes to absorb the remain
  ing water. You should be able to hear the different
  stages of cooking: at first, the rice bubbles, but when
  all the water has been absorbed, it begins to hiss
  Never remove the lid during cooking if you want the
  very best rice.
- Once the rice has cooked, remove the lid, drape a
  teacloth over the top of the pan and let it cool for
  10–15 minutes.

1 The cooked and cooled rice is poured into a
hangiri.

■ Pour the rice into a *hangiri* (cedarwood rice-cooling tub) or other non-metallic container. Spread it out evenly with a *shamoji* (rice-paddle) or large wooden spoon.

■ Run the *shamoji* through the rice as though you were ploughing a field, first left-to-right and then top-to-bottom, again and again. This is to separate the grains. As you do so, add the *sushi-zu*; ⅔cup/150ml/5fl oz will treat 1½–2lb/750g–1kg/1½–2lb *uncooked* rice. Do not add too much: the rice should just stick together without being mushy.

■ At the same time, you need to fan the rice to cool it and help it separate – the action will also add a gloss to the grains. Unless you have three hands, you will need an assistant with an *uchiwa* (a fan) or an un-romantic but equally effective piece of cardboard. It takes about 10 minutes to get the rice thoroughly mixed and down to room temperature.

2 Using a *shamoji*, or large wooden spoon, quickly and lightly toss and cut the rice to separate the individual grains.

If you cannot get ready-made *sushi-zu* (sushi vinegar), dissolve 5tbsp/75ml/2½oz sugar in a little more than 5tbsp/75ml/2½fl oz rice vinegar with 2–4 tsp/10–20ml/2–4tsp salt (the higher quantity is more traditional). You will have to first heat the vinegar to get the sugar to dissolve, then cool rapidly by plunging the bowl into cold water, to avoid distilling off the vinegar.

3 At the same time add the *sushi-zu*.

NIGIRI-ZUSHI TECHNIQUE

'*Nigiri*' literally means 'squeezing', and that is what you do. Left-handers should follow a mirror image of the sequence given below; Japan is a strongly right- handed society.

There are several classic shapes for making the 'pillow' of rice, including *kushi-gata* or *rikyu-gata* (elongated dome), *ogi-gata* (fan shape, a flattened version of *kushi-gata*), *funa-gata* (boat-shaped, with a flat top, a curved bottom, and punt-like squared-off bow and transom, as shown here), *tawara-gata* (lightly compressed to give a fat sausage shape like a rice bale or long cotton bale), and *hako-gata* (box-shaped). The first two are the most usual, and the last two are rare.

I Pick up the topping with the left hand. Pick up a ball of rice with your right hand; the rice-tub should be on your right side. Round the ball of rice against the wall of the rice-tub. At this stage, uncompressed, the ball should be around the size of a golf ball or ping-pong ball.

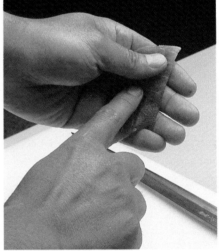

2 With the rice ba in the palm of yo right hand, pick a dab of *wasabi* your right inde finger and smear on the centre of t underside of t topping.

3 Put the rice ba onto the toppin Keeping the finge of the left hand fla lightly press the ri under the toppin Your thumb w leave a small depre sion in the ball.

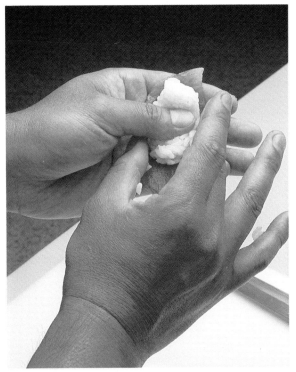

Squeeze the sides with your right hand.

5 Curling your left hand around the sushi, with the left thumb as shown, press down with the first two fingers of your right hand to squeeze it flat.

6 Transfer the sushi to your other hand.

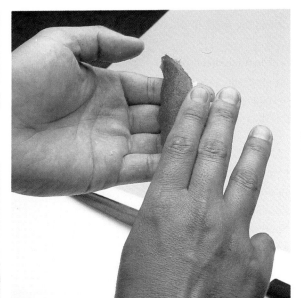

7 Replace it in the left hand, but end-over-end: the part that was squeezed by your thumb is now at the open side of the hand.

9 Roll the sushi from the cup of your hand to the fingers, so the topping is on top.

8 Repeat step 5 above: this evens up the other end of the sushi.

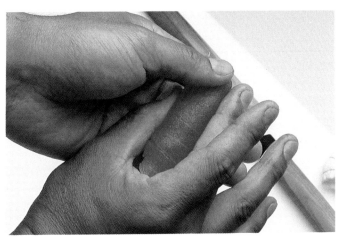

10 Give a final squeeze to even out the shape.

MAKI TECHNIQUE

Gunkan-maki ('battleship sushi') has already been mentioned; the technique for making them is shown in Roe (pages 68 and 69).

Temaki is made on a strip of *nori* (seaweed paper) 1in/2.5cm/1in wide; a little sushi rice and some topping are laid on top, and the roll is wrapped and stuck as for *gunkan-maki*. This technique is shown on pages 88 and 89.

Other forms of *maki* are made with a *makisu* (bamboo rolling mat). The tight-rolled *maki* include small *maki* or *hoso-maki*, as illustrated here; fat *futo-maki* (page 56); 'inside out' *maki*, like the California Roll (page 50) and garnished *maki* like the Rainbow Roll (page 66).

The basic technique for *hoso-maki* is this:

When cutting a roll, if you have any particularly ingredients which might make neat cutting difficult, such as carrot or *kampyō*, cut down with a steady slicing motion until you encounter resistance, then hit the back of the blade smartly with your free hand to complete the cut.

1 Put a half sheet *no[ri]* on the *makisu*, the[n] cover with a layer [of] sushi rice abo[ut] ⅜in/1cm thick. (all the way to t[he] sides but leave t[he] top and bottom of t[he] *nori* uncovered.

2 Put the topping or[?] the rice; sever[al] toppings are oft[en] mixed. This is bu[r]dock root, which [is] hot and crunchy is available cann[ed] in some Orient[al] stores). *Goma* (se[s]ame seeds) a[re] added here f[or] flavour. If you we[re] making a fish ro[ll] you would a[dd] *wasabi* (Japane[se] horseradish).

3 Roll the *maki* up the *makisu*, starti[ng] from the edge ne[ar]est you.

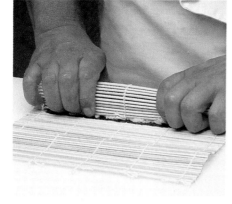

4 Stop just before you complete the roll, to pull the end of the *makisu* out of the way.

5 Finish rolling with the *makisu*. Compress the roll: some people square the roll, while others leave it round.

6 Push in the ends if they are untidy.

7 Wet the knife in a bowl containing vinegar-water and a slice of lemon.

8 Tap the butt of the knife on the table to spread the vinegar-water over the blade's surface.

9 Cut the roll in half and lay the two halves side by side.

10 Divide each half into 3 equal sections, giving 6 slices in all.

1 The *awabi* does not look promising.

2 Cut out the mouth parts.

  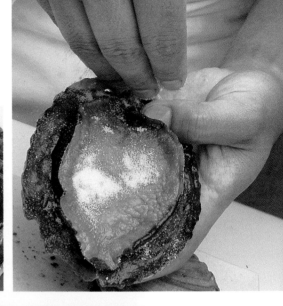

4 Carefully cut the *awabi* out of the shell with a sharp knife.

5 Remove the entrails. The stomach, sliced raw and mixed with *ponzu* (citrus vinegar; page 58) and a little spring onion (scallion) is regarded as a delicacy. Some people even eat the rest of the entrails, though these are normally cooked.

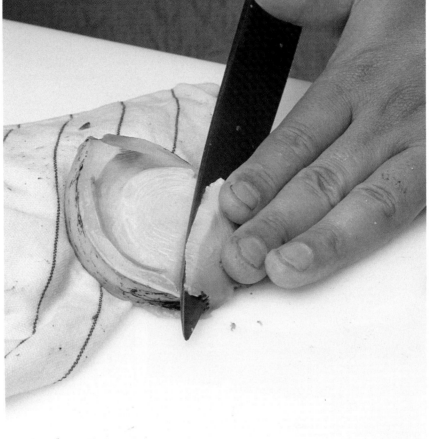

3 Sprinkle generous with salt. Tap th shell to make su the salt penetrat everywhere. After minute or so, th flesh will be contra ted and rigid.

6 Scrub the main bo of the *awabi* with brush and plenty salt. It is now pe fectly clean.

7 Remove the da fringe around th edge of the fles On a large abalo this will be t tough to be edible

8 If the *awabi* is b enough, remove t small muscle on t for the very be sushi. Otherwis slice the whole fi diagonally.

ABALONE
(*AWABI*)

Awabi (abalone) is regarded as one of the great delicacies of sushi. Before about 1950, it was normally
cooked before serving, but today the most highly prized
form is the fresh, raw *awabi*.

The smaller the *awabi*, the more tender the flesh.
Awabi of 4in/10cm or under can be sliced whole: bigger
ones are prepared as shown.

Abalone are widely
distributed in
temperate and
tropical seas,
especially around
Australia. They are
also found along the
West Coast of North
America and off
Japan, the Channel
Islands, the west
coast of France, and
in the
Mediterranean, as
well as China and the
Canary Islands. They
are reckoned to be at
their best in April,
May and June. They
live on the seabed
near the *kombu* and
nori on which they
feed – an apparent
example of
predestination . . .
The Sea Cradle, Gum
Boot or Giant Chiton
(related to the limpet)
can be prepared as
for *awabi*.

1 Spread a thin layer (about ⅜in/1cm) of sushi rice on a half sheet of *nori* (seaweed paper). Sprinkle with *goma* (sesame seeds).

2 Turn the whole thing over and smear a little *wasabi* (Japanese horseradish) on the *nori*.

3 Strips of finely sliced cucumber and avocado are added first in the middle.

4 Crab meat completes the contents.

5 Roll the whole thing up Swiss-roll style, using your fingers.

8 A garnish of smelt roe is not essential, but it does make the roll more colourful.

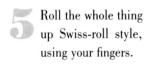

6 Place a piece of cling-film (plastic wrap) over it.

7 With the *makisu* form the roll tightly. Before the invention of cling-film, a wet *makisu* was used; cling-film is easier.

CALIFORNIA ROLL
AND
VEGETABLE ROLL

As its name suggests, California Roll is hardly a classical sushi recipe. It is, however, extremely popular on the West Coast of the United States, and has made progress not only on the East Coast but even in Tokyo. It is a superb blend of textures: cooked crab, avocado and cucumber. Also, of course, it appeals to people who want to try sushi but are not sure about raw fish.

Although it is quite possible to make a *hoso-maki* roll in this way, there is not much space available for filling if you do. Consequently, it is usual to make these rolls inside-out.

Inside-out Vegetable Rolls are more traditional than California Rolls, but generally less popular in the West. Instead of the cucumber-avocado-crab filling, the traditional ingredients are cucumber or seasoned *kampyō* (pages 38 and 39). You may wish to try other ingredients, including finely sliced carrot, mange-touts (snow peas) and even cream cheese.

For presentation, the California Roll is carefully sliced into six pieces. The end pieces, with the ends protruding, are normally placed in the middle.

CLAMS

Various kinds of clam are popular in Japan, though they are not so highly regarded in the West.

Akagai (ark shell) is often called the king of sushi bivalves, and is correspondingly expensive; only the most expensive places buy it other than frozen, and in the United States it is only available cooked and frozen.

The fresh shellfish is 3–4in/7.5–10cm across, and is usually washed in vinegar before being cut up. Various different parts are prized, including the adductor muscle (*hashira*) and the threadlike filaments which attach the flesh to the shell (*himo*). The red colouring is due to haemoglobin, the same agent which colours human blood.

The *aoyagi* (round clam), is also known as the *bakagai* or *'fool shellfish'*. Formerly served lightly cooked, it is now eaten raw; as with the *akagai*, the adductor muscle is highly prized.

The long, muscular siphon of the *mirugai* (horse-clam, geoduck) is used in sushi: the *himo* is sometimes eaten raw, but the rest of the flesh is really only suitable for making clam chowder or clam stuffing. *Miru-kui or miru-gai* are found off the coast of Japan and the north-western coast of the United States.

The foot of the cockle, *tori-gai*, is also highly regarded. The name comes from the dark end of the meat, which is said to resemble a chicken's beak, and from the taste, which some say resembles chicken: *tori* means 'chicken' and *kai* (changing to *gai* in a compound word) means 'shellfish'. Cockles are traditionally used with shrimp in Edomae *chirashi-zushi*.

Many types of shellfish can be prepared like this; ask your fishmonger what is in season in your area. Small clams – cherrystones and smaller – are often used whole in *gunkan-maki*, while larger ones are sliced either raw or cooked.

1 *Miru-gai* means 'a shellfish to be seen' or 'something remarkable'. The siphon is removed, and boiling water is poured over it to loosen the skin.

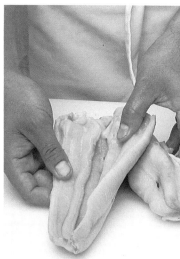

2 The skinned and cleaned siphon looks very much more appetizing.

3 As usual, the flesh is cut on the bias. The sliced flesh is hammered with the very bottom of the knife blade to tenderize it.

4 The strip of *nori* wrapped around the sushi is for traction, not culinary variety. Like other types of slippery fish, the *mirugai* might slip off the rice if not secured.

E G G P A N C A K E
(*T a m a g o*)

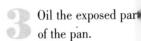

Tamago, or sweetened egg pancake, is traditionally eaten at the end of a sushi meal as sort of a dessert. It is cooked in a rectangular omelette pan. In a bowl, mix the following (do not attempt to reduce quantities – a 10 egg omelette would be even easier to prepare).

INGREDIENTS
⅓ cup/75ml/2½fl oz *dashi* (see page 36)

⅓ cup/75g/2½oz sugar

1½tsp/7.5ml/1½tsp soy sauce

1½tsp/7.5ml/1½tsp *sake*

½tsp/2.5ml/½tsp salt

5 eggs

Vegetable oil for frying

PREPARATION
- Combine the first 5 ingredients over a low heat, stirring until the sugar and salt are dissolved. Let the stock (broth) cool to room temperature.
- Beat the eggs, introducing as little air as possible: you do not want a fluffy mixture.
- Combine the beaten eggs and the cooled stock.
- In a lightly oiled pan, pour one quarter of the mixtue, tilting the pan to coat the base evenly. Cook until the egg is barely set, pricking any bubbles with a long chopstick. This is where the difference from a western omelette starts to become really obvious.

1 Fold the omelette in half.

2 Leave the other half of the pan empty.

3 Oil the exposed part of the pan.

4 Slide the omelette over to the newly oiled part and oil the other half of the pan.

5 Pour in the same amount of mixture, one quarter of original volume, or one third of what is left.

6 Lift omelette to allow uncooked mixture to run underneath.

7 When this is cooked, fold and repeat the process, adding more egg mixture; then with the last portion of the egg mixture, repeat it again.

8 Cook the block a little longer to caramelize the sugar on the surface, then turn out onto a flat surface to cool. Cut into about 8 'bricks' when cool.

Tamago-zushi *consists of a piece of sweet omelette on rice, usually secured with a 'belt' of* nori *(seaweed paper). Alternatively, and more traditionally, serve two blocks per person with a little well-drained grated* daikon *as a garnish.*

LARGE ROLLS (Futo-maki)

Futo-maki can contain almost anything, though they are usually vegetarian. The main differences between these and the smaller maki are their size, and the fact that the nori is rolled into the roll in a spiral.

Typical ingredients include boiled spinach, cucumber, kampyō (dried gourd), sliced shiitake mushrooms, tamago (egg pancake), bamboo shoot and lotus root. There is also a form of prepared cooked fish called oboro, which is either bought ready-made or can be prepared at home.

Oboro

To prepare oboro at home, boil white fish until thoroughly cooked, then remove the skin and bones. Dry by squeezing in a cloth. Pound the flesh in a mortar (or use a food processor, though the result will not be quite the same), adding a few drops of cochineal or other red food colour to tint the oboro pink. Cook the paste in a heavy saucepan with small amounts of sugar, sake and salt, stirring constantly until all the moisture has evaporated.

1 Use a full sheet of nori (seaweed paper), not a half-sheet. Cover the whole sheet, except for about ⅜in/1cm at one end, with a layer of sushi rice about ⅜in/1cm thick. On the bare strip of nori at the end, crush a couple of grains of rice to act as an adhesive. Place bands of whatever ingredients you want to use across the short dimension of the sheet. Here, we begin with spinach.

2 Tamago (egg pancake) and oboro have then been added. Finally, some kampyō (dried gourd) is used.

3 Roll up the futo-maki with your fingers – carefully! The bare ends of nori should be tucked into the body of the roll.

4 Compress the roll with the makisu, pressing in the ends. You may also shape the futo-maki, making it slightly oval, or squared-off. To serve, slice in half, then put the 2 halves together and slice into 4 segments.

HALIBUT (*Hirame*)
AND
SALMON (*Sake*)

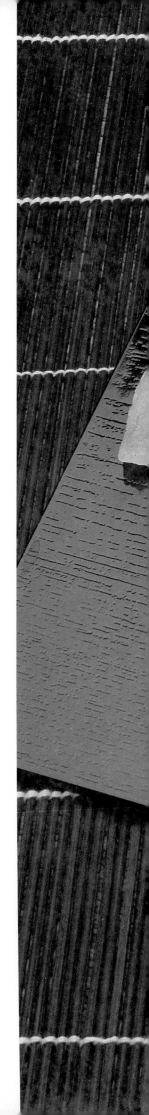

Various types of flatfish are served as sushi, but they are all served the same way. Depending on where you live, the same or very similar fishes may be called halibut, plaice or flounder – though the halibut is normally much bigger. Flatfish sometimes appear on sushi bar menus under the unappetizing name of 'fluke'.

The Japanese flatfish is small, more like a plaice or flounder, but the big *hirame* (halibut) is prepared in the same way. You get much more *engawa* (prized meat next to side fins; page 29) from a *hirame*!

Most species are reckoned to be at their best in winter, with autumn as the second season of choice.

The flesh may simply be sliced and served as *nigiri-zushi* with no further preparation, or it may be briefly marinated in a sauce made of spring onion (scallion), *momigi oroshi* (hot-pepper paste in vinegar) and *ponzu* (citrus vinegar).

Ponzu is obtainable ready-to-use from Japanese shops, or you can make a substitute by adding 1 cup/250ml/8fl oz orange juice and the juice of 1 lemon to 4½ cups/1 litre/35fl oz *su* (rice vinegar).

At the Yamato, *ponzu* is not used alone. To make a useful sauce, which can be used with fish or as a basis for powerful soup (*suimono*), bring 4½ cups/1 litre/35fl oz *ponzu* to the boil with *kombu* and *katsuo-bushi* (page 36), add an equal volume of soy sauce and ½ cup/125ml/4fl oz *mirin*, then strain.

Where salmon is served as sashimi, the presentation is much the same as for flatfish. In Japan, salmon is hardly ever served raw, and California is probably the only area where it is really popular. Cod and rock cod can be served the same way. Shark could also be prepared by the same techniques, but most people find it too fishy tasting.

Hirame *and salmon served as* nigiri-zushi.

DEEP·FRIED TOFU (*Inari*)

Inari are somewhat bland pockets of tofu which have been deep fried, then braised. They are stuffed with sushi rice, with or without the addition of *goma* (sesame seeds) or *gari* (pickled ginger). They are something of an acquired taste, but they are economical and they keep well, making them popular as a light packed lunch.

Age (tofu pouches) are bought already deep-fried; they are available frozen or refrigerated in some Oriental markets. They are very perishable and should be used within a couple of days if they are not kept frozen. They are first blanched in boiling water for a few seconds to remove excess oil, then drained and dried on absorbent paper. While they are still warm, cut in half.

To create the pocket, put a half-pouch in the palm of one hand, and slap it smartly with the other hand; loosening the middle. You can now open it up gently to create a deep pouch.

INGREDIENTS OF
BRAISING STOCK FOR *AGE*

This is enough stock (broth) for 8 half pouches

½ cup/125ml/4fl oz *dashi* (page 36)

heaped ½ cup/120g/4oz sugar

3tbsp/45ml/1½fl oz soy sauce

2tbsp/30ml/1fl oz *sake*

METHOD

■ Mix all the ingredients together in a large saucepan, heating until the sugar is dissolved. Braise the pouches in this for 6–7 minutes, basting frequently to avoid scorching. Cool to room temperature, without draining. When cool, drain.

The name *inari* comes from folk-lore. The fox which supposedly guarded the temples of the god Inari was said to be especially fond of *age*, so sushi made from *age* are named after the god. Sometimes, they are called 'Fox Sushi', from the same legend.

1 Open the braised pouch.

2 Fill with sushi rice and compress the rice with the thumb.

3 Present the *inari* with the flap tucked under.

MACKEREL (Saba)
AND
GIZZARD SHAD (Kohada)

Saba (mackerel) and *kohada* (gizzard shad) a member of the herring family, are prepared in much the same way. They are both examples of *hikari-mono*, 'things that shine' – fish with silvery skin, normally marinated.

The *kohada* is somewhat confusingly known by different names as it matures: initially *kohada*, then *nakazumi* or *shinko* and, when fully mature, *konoshiro*.

Both *saba* and *kohada* are filleted using the three-piece system (page 28). The fillets are salted generously, then left for anything from four hours upwards (*saba*) or an hour or two (*kohada*). The salt is washed off before the next step.

Next, they are marinated in vinegar which has been sweetened with 2tbsp/30g/1oz sugar to 1 cup/250ml/8fl oz vinegar. *Saba* is typically marinated for 30 minutes–1 hour, though some people prefer even longer – a day or more. *Kohada* is marinated for a shorter time, perhaps 15 minutes.

In general, the fresher the fish, the less time it is marinated: fresh-caught *kohada* may be salted for as little as 30 minutes and marinated for as little as 5–10 minutes.

Kohada *and* saba *served as* nigiri-zushi.

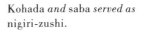

1 The *saba* is a larger fish than the *kohada*, and is normally salted and marinated for longer.

2 Unlike the *saba*, which is normally cut into many slices, the *kohada* is normally cut into only 2 pieces.

3 The skin of *hikari-mono* is usually slashed, to show the contrast between the silvery skin and the flesh underneath.

Other typically Japanese *hikari-mono* include *sayori* (halfbeak) and *kisu* (sillago), but most small fish which travel in glittering shoals can be prepared in the same way. Examples might include herring, fresh sardines, fresh anchovies, fresh pilchards and smelts.

he sliced tako *is*
ormally secured to the rice
ith a 'belt' of nori
eaweed paper). This is not
> much for flavour, as to
op the shiny slices from
ipping off the sushi.

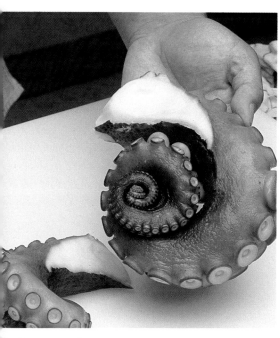

Even quite large tentacles can make good sushi.

Cut through the tentacles on the bias. Using a very sharp knife, a 'wiggling' cut will produce a slice that is easier to cut and attractive. Cut off the dark upper surface of the tentacle, but leave the sucker side.

OCTOPUS
(*Tako*)

Tako (octopus) is *always* lightly cooked; it is never served raw. In order to get really fresh *tako*, it is as well to start with a live one or at least with one that you know has not been dead for long. Like shellfish, a *tako* that has gone off can have very unpleasant effects on the system, but it is not necessarily easy to tell the vintage of a dead *tako*. Look for a pale grey speckled skin and tentacles which bounce when shaken.

Preparing a *tako* from scratch is not as difficult (or as unattractive) as you might think. The entrails are in the head, which is turned inside-out for cleaning; the eyes and beak are best cut out with kitchen shears. Clean the fish thoroughly, using lots of salt and fresh water to remove slime and sand, and pay special attention to the suckers on the tentacles.

Lower the *tako* slowly, tentacles first, into a large pan of vigourously boiling water until the tentacles are red and resilient. The tentacles are what is served on sushi.

RAINBOW ROLL

The Rainbow Roll is the most colourful of the inside-out rolls which have become popular since the 1950s. The only easy way to make them is with the aid of cling film (plastic wrap). Before the advent of cling film, they were sometimes made using a cloth or a second wetted *makisu* (bamboo rolling mat), but the whole process is much easier with cling film!

The technique and inside ingredients are the same as for the California Roll (page 50). In fact, at the Yamato, the Rainbow Roll is on the menu as a California Special Roll.

Once you have your basic inside-out roll, place strips of different-coloured fish and avocado on top of the roll; they must be very thinly sliced, but thick enough to show the colour. Garnish with sesame seeds if you like; black ones are dramatic.

Put more cling film around the whole thing, and roll once again in the *makisu*. Remove the cling film and slice – or, if you are feeling cowardly, remove the cling film *after* slicing.

1 Choose the fish for colour: white fish like halibut, creamy-coloured fish like yellowtail, fresh orange or smoked salmon, red bonita. Slice very thinly.

2 Alternate the colours for maximum effect.

3 Squeeze in a *makisu* after wrapping it with cling-film.

The version shown here is garnished with the yolk of a quail egg, somewhat after the fashion of steak tartare, but this is an unusual refinement which is rarely seen in Japan.

1 To build a *gunkan-maki*, take a standard-sized piece of sushi rice and put it in the middle of a long strip of *nori* (seaweed paper).

2 When you roll the *nori*, make it slightly skewed. This is not just to appeal to the Japanese love of asymmetry, it makes the roll easier to build.

3 Tuck the edge of the *nori* underneath, where it will stick to the rice.

4 Fill the completed *gunkan-maki* with roe; this is salmon roe.

ROE

Many kinds of roe (fish eggs) are used in sushi. Because they are soft, they are mostly made into *gunkan-maki* ('battleship' sushi).

The most common variety is probably *ikura* (golden-red salmon roe). This is sold ready-packed, like caviare, and is one of the largest of roes. If it is exposed to the air for too long, it loses its glossy texture and bright colour, but these can be restored by soaking the roe in *sake* for a short while. If the *ikura* is bought with the ovarian membrane still around the roe, it is known as *suzuko*.

Tarako (salted cod roe) is a popular topping; the roe is reddish-brown and significantly smaller than salmon roe. *Tarako* is frequently artificially coloured a vivid red or a virulent orange.

Kazu-no-ko (salted herring roe) is very highly regarded, though arguably as a fertility symbol rather than for its taste. It is extremely expensive: the popular name of 'yellow diamonds' refers as much to the price as to the colour and the symbolism. Immature eggs are less colourful and lustrous, and command a lower price because they do not taste as good.

Instead of being extracted from the live herring, *komochi kombu* is kelp *(kombu)* on which the herring has spawned; a strip is placed atop a finger of sushi rice. Both *kazu-no-ko* and *komochi kombu* are desalted by soaking in water for at least two hours. Perhaps surprisingly, adding a little salt to the water seems to speed the desalting process.

Lumpfish roe and true (sturgeon) caviare can also be used. Unsalted fresh caviare would probably be delicious, but the likelihood of finding it is vanishingly small.

SCALLOPS (Hotate-gai) AND OYSTERS (Kaki)

A swimming *hotate-gai* (scallop) is a remarkable sight. Instead of remaining peacefully on the sea floor, as most of us expect bivalves to do, it opens and closes its shell to move at quite a fair rate. The adductor muscle which enables it to do this is appropriately large, and is sliced for use in sushi. As with the *awabi* (abalone), the rest of the *hotate-gai* is also eaten, but it is not normally used in sushi.

In Japan, *hotate-gai* farming is quite common, most frequent around Hokkaido and Aomori in the north.

Most sushi bars normally use frozen *hotate-gai*. Smaller ones are usually cut into small chunks and served as *gunan-maki* ('battleship' sushi), but the larger ones can be prepared as *nigiri-zushi* (finger sushi). The adductor muscle as removed from a large *hotate-gai* can be 1–2in/ 2.5–5cm in diameter, and anything from ½–2½in/ 1–6cm long. It is ivory white and sits smack in the middle of the shell, surrounded by the rest of the shellfish. Like many shellfish, *hotate-gai* is tenderest when raw and it becomes increasingly tough when cooked. Five minutes' cooking can reduce the tenderest one to the consistency of India-rubber.

The *kaki* (oyster) is more staid, and sits peacefully on its oyster bed. As in the West, *kaki* are often served in Japan on the half shell, but whole small *kaki* or chopped large *kaki* may also appear in the form of *gunkan-maki*.

Kaki served on the half shell garnished with salmon roe, and hotate-gai served as gunkan-maki

SCATTERED SUSHI
(*Chirashi·zushi*)

The *chirashi-zushi* (scattered sushi) illustrated here is the *Kanto-fu Chirashi-zushi*; Kanto is the eastern part of Japan, and it is where *chirashi-zushi* originated. It consists of nothing more than a bed of plain sushi rice, on which are placed various kinds of fish, together with thick *tamago* (omelette), *kampyō* (dried gourd) and *shiitake* mushrooms.

Another form of *chirashi-zushi* is made by mixing all the ingredients together with *gomoku-zushi*, though in western Japan (Kansai) it is known simply as *chirashi-*

zushi again. Another name for *gomoku-zushi* is therefore *Kansai-fu Chirashi-zushi*.

Because there are so many ways of making it, preparation of *chirashi-zushi* is more a question of state of mind than of following a recipe. Just keep experimenting until you find the mixture that suits you best. One of the simplest forms of *gomoku-zushi*, for example, is *kani* (crab) *chirashi-zushi*, a rice salad mixed with the crab. For ½lb/225g/½lb crab meat (sprinkled with the juice of half a small lemon), use the following quantities:

INGREDIENTS

2½ cups/500g/1lb cooked sushi rice (pages 42 and 43)

2 cucumbers

2 large *shiitake* mushrooms, prepared as on page 38

2oz/60g/2oz *renkon* (lotus root), peeled, available from Oriental shops tinned

3 tamago (page 54), thinly sliced

reduced *dashi* (pages 36 and 37)

½ tsp/2.5 ml/½ tsp salt

1tsp/5ml/1tsp sugar

PREPARATION

■ Slice the cucumbers thinly and reduce their moisture by 'sweating' them under a fine sprinkling of salt for a few minutes, then washing in fresh water and squeezing dry. Soak the lotus root in vinegared water for 10 minutes.

■ Boil just enough water to cover all the slices and add a pinch of salt and a dash of water. Blanch the slices for about 30 seconds, then drain and marinate in reduced *dashi* (pages 36 and 37) or water with the salt and sugar.

■ Mix all the ingredients together, reserving a few for garnish. Or, use *kamaboko* (fish cake) or more crab as a garnish. Or, garnish with boiled prawns (shrimp), sliced eel, gizzard, shad, tuna and squid, *tamago* (omelette), more *shiitake* and lotus root, prepared as above and 1 cucumber, prepared as above. *Gari* and *wasabi* can be added to taste, and of course you can always add *kampyō* to any *chirashi-zushi*.

■ Other forms of *chirashi-zushi* are made with deep-fried beancurd, green beans, bamboo shoots and even chicken.

SEA BREAM (*Tai*)

The *tai* (sea bream) used for sushi may be served without further treatment, but they are often served partially cooked on the skin side. The cooking is accomplished by pouring boiling water over the fish.

The traditional way to do it is by preparing the fish in the usual *sanmai-oroshi* fashion (page 28), placing a cloth over the skin side, and pouring boiling water over it. If you are in a hurry, pouring boiling water directly over the fillet is quicker and easier, and produces an almost identical effect.

Another way to serve *tai* is to clean and bone a whole fish, and then to serve it with the body cavity stuffed with sushi rice. Because *tai* is regarded as one of the very finest fish for sushi, it is often used as the centrepiece in a sushi boat or other spectacular set piece.

Sliced, filleted tai *served as* nigiri-zushi.

1 *Tai* are not large fish: their bigger relatives, such as the grouper, are not usually prepared this way.

2 Carefully remove the fillets *sanmai-oroshi* style (page 28) if the fish is to be used as a garnish. (This is the same fish that appears in the sushi boat on the cover and title page.)

3 A tea-cloth is ideal for wrapping.

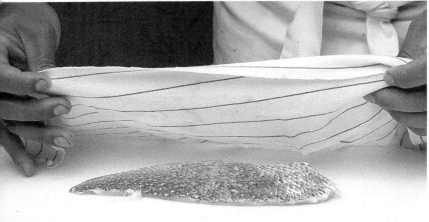

4 The difference may not be clear in reproduction, but the fish that has been treated with boiling water has a duller, whiter skin than the silvery untreated fillet below.

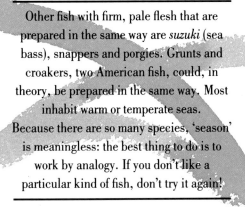

Other fish with firm, pale flesh that are prepared in the same way are *suzuki* (sea bass), snappers and porgies. Grunts and croakers, two American fish, could, in theory, be prepared in the same way. Most inhabit warm or temperate seas. Because there are so many species, 'season' is meaningless: the best thing to do is to work by analogy. If you don't like a particular kind of fish, don't try it again!

SEA EEL (Anago)

AND

EEL (Unagi)

Unagi (eel) is cooked before being used to make sushi. The *anago* is the famous conger eel, but you want only small specimens. The giant mankillers do not taste so good, and are in any case inconvenient to handle and cook. A good *unagi* is even smaller, and weighs only 5–6oz/150–180g/5–6oz.

Filleting *unagi* is different from filleting other fish. The easiest way to do it is to pin the head down on a chopping board, with the backbone towards you. Make an incision with a sharp knife just above the backbone, behind the head, and cut from head to tail. Lift this fillet carefully and flip it over onto the chopping board.

Cut through the backbone just behind the head, and holding the knife parallel to the chopping board, slide it under the backbone from head to tail. Remove the backbone and entrails and scrape the slimy skin with the back of the knife. Rinse and drain.

Remove any remaining bones with a very sharp knife. even commercial fillets may require this treatment.

To cook *anago*, braise it, skin side down, 7–8 minutes in a boiling mixture of equal quanitites (by volume) of soy sauce, *sake*, *mirin* and sugar. For still more flavour, grill (broil) the fillets after they have cooled.

Grill *unagi* fillets skin side first on a skewer, in kebab-size chunks. Next, steam the grilled *unagi* for about 5 minutes, then drain. Baste with a sauce of *mirin* and sugar – about 1 part sugar to 3 parts *mirin*, then grill again, basting 2 or 3 times while grilling.

If you continue to cook *anago* in the liquid mentioned above, until the sauce begins to reduce, you will get a very thick, syrupy, strong-flavoured dark-brown sauce called *tsu-me*. Continue to cook the stock, adding a little more soy sauce, sugar and mirin if it gets too dry. The resulting sauce, which is also thickened by the gelatine from the *anago*, is frequently used to dribble over different kinds of sushi.

1 Scrape the skin with a knife to remove the slime. The direction of movement in this picture is from left (as you look at it) to right.

2 Slice out the ribs.

3 Remove the backbone.

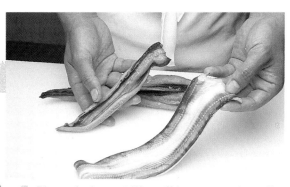

4 The cooked *unagi* fillet will be very much smaller than the uncooked version.

SEA URCHIN
(*Uni*)

The interior parts of the prickly *uni* (sea urchin) are a delicacy in many parts of the world; the roe, which clings to the inside of the shell in five top-to-bottom strips, is what is normally eaten. Some people eat the meat as well.

Uni probably spoil faster than any other kind of shellfish, so unless you get live ones (which normally means catching them yourself), it is as well to buy prepared roe, sold in a box as shown. Alternatively, bottled *uni* or *neri uni* (sea urchin roe) is good – unless you compare it with the original. The difference is analogous to the difference between fresh and canned pineapple.

To prepare fresh *uni*, split the fragile shell in half with a heavy, sharp knife; smaller or blunt knives will crush the shell rather than cutting through. The watery flesh and the mouth parts in the middle are discarded. The roe of the male is yellow and edible; the orange roe of the female is more highly prized.

Because uni *is so soft, it is normally made into* gunkan-maki *('battleship' sushi). In the United States,* uni-maki *are sometimes garnished with a quail's egg.*

Ready-prepared uni *can be purchased in a box.*

PRAWNS (*Ebi*)

Ebi (prawns/shrimp) is traditionally served cooked; only the very freshest 'sweet' prawn (shrimp) is served raw.

The trick with cooked *ebi* is to keep them straight while they are cooking, and this is done with a very thin skewer inserted as shown. Stainless steel skewers are probably the most convenient, though bamboo skewers are more traditional. If you use bamboo skewers, wet them before use.

Wash the *ebi* thoroughly, then remove the vein with a toothpick inserted between the joints and the shell. Skewer the *ebi*, and drop them into boiling water. The *ebi* should sink at first, then rise to the surface when they are cooked. Scoop the *ebi* out, and drop them into ice water; this not only improves the colour, but also makes it easier to remove the skewer. Twist the skewer as you remove it.

Peel the *ebi*, removing the legs and head but leaving the very tip of the tail intact.

Slice along the bottom of the *ebi* and 'butterfly' it, turning it inside out. Cover and refrigerate until used – and use quickly, because it is not easy to tell when cooked *ebi* have gone off.

Various kinds of prawns (shrimp) are prepared for sushi. They have to be big enough to make it worthwhile, but small enough not to be unwieldy – no one makes crayfish sushi! Sometimes, you may find the ugly-looking but delicious mantis shrimp, which can be served raw or cooked.

Raw prawns are peeled and tailed in the same way as cooked ones, albeit with slightly more difficulty. You can use frozen prawns this way, but they will need to be expensive, individually frozen prawns; others will be too watery and flavourless.

---

1 Anti-clockwise from bottom left: raw *ebi* tail with bamboo skewer for cooking; cooked *ebi* with skewer; cooked *ebi* after removal of the skewer.

2 Peel the *ebi*. Traditionally, a small part of the tail tip is left on; cut at an angle like this.

3 Slice into the belly of the *ebi* without cutting all the way through to the back.

4 Turn the *ebi* inside out to create a 'butterfly' shrimp.

SMOKED SALMON

Smoked salmon is not exactly a traditional Japanese ingredient – indeed, it is commonly known in Japan by its English name – but, like so many other non-traditional ingredients, it works very well.

Use the fine, translucent type of slow-smoked salmon that is common in England (Scotch or Canadian smoked salmon), rather than the coarse chunks which are sometimes prepared in the United States. Slice finely, and use as sushi on Rainbow Rolls (page 66), as a garnish with roe or *uni* (sea urchin) or in any other way you think fit.

At the Yamato, a popular way to serve smoked salmon is in a Kosher Roll, with cream cheese and, according to taste, either *wakegi* (spring onion) or cucumber.

At home, you can prepare Kosher Roll using economical smoked salmon pieces or pâte rather than sides or large fillets of smoked salmon. It is also an excellent way to serve sushi to people who do not like, cannot eat, or are afraid of raw fish.

1 Using the basic technique for an inside-out roll (page 50), begin with cucumber or spring onion (scallion) or both.

2 Next, add strips of smoked salmon. Be fairly generous or the delicate taste will be overwhelmed by the other ingredients.

3 Cut cream cheese into strips about ¼ sq in/.5 sq cm and put them alongside the smoked salmon strips, then roll.

4 Cut the roll in half and put the 2 pieces side by side, then cut twice more to get 6 pieces.

SPICY SUSHI

With spicy sushi, it is as well to use the stronger-flavoured fish such as tuna, bonita and yellowtail or even shark. Otherwise, it is all too easy for the fish to be overwhelmed by the spicing. If you use sesame oil, though, you should beware of the fatter belly cuts of fish, or the result may be unpalatably greasy.

Traditionally, *wasabi* (Japanese horseradish) and vinegar were the only spices used in making sushi. In the last few years, however, spicy sushi has become increasingly popular.

The main spices used are hot red-pepper paste – which is literally made of hot red peppers, salt and water and nothing else – and in some restaurants sesame oil. *Wakegi* (spring onions/scallions) are also used to liven up bland food, and the taste of *daikon* (white radish) sprouts is very memorable. *Daikon* sprouts resemble large mustard and cress, but are much hotter and spicier.

Unless you are a lover of hot foods, you should use most of these sparingly at first, but it is very easy to build up a tolerance for hot food, and subsequently to serve delicacies to your guests which cause their eyes to cross and their tongues to hang out!

Rather than *nigiri-zushi* (finger sushi), where the marinade could easily burn the lips or tongue, it is usual to make spicy sushi in the form of *maki*. That way, the flavours are well mingled before the spices hit the taste-buds. You can make spicy *maki* either inside-out or as regular small *maki*. Two popular forms of spicy sushi at the Yamato are:

Spicy Kosher Roll

The Kosher Roll is made in the way described under salmon (page 82), but with *wakegi*, a liberal sprinkling of *goma* (sesame seeds) and the cheese as well as the salmon marinated in a mixture of hot-pepper sauce and soy sauce. The flavour can be so powerful you could probably miss out the smoked salmon and nobody would notice!

Marinated spicy tuna is here used in a small maki.

Spicy Tuna

1 Mix together in a bowl soy sauce and hot-pepper paste.

2 Add a tiny amount of chopped *wakegi*. Add the tuna and marinate.

SQUID (*IKA*)

Traditionally, *ika* (squid) is a very important sushi topping – but until recently, it was always cooked. Raw *ika* is a pallid white, with a texture that does not appeal to everyone. Cooked *ika* has a purplish-red skin, somewhat resembling cooked octopus. Many modern sushi restaurants serve both.

Unlike *tako* (octopus), where the tentacles are the main attraction, the outer body of the *ika* is what is usually served in sushi.

To prepare a fresh *ika*, grip the body in one hand and the tentacles with the other; salting your hands liberally will make it easier to get a good grip. Pull the body and the tentacles apart. The tentacles will pull away, complete with the entrails.

Clean the body well with plenty of salt. Pull off the fins and the thick skin, then rinse and dry. The *ika* may be served raw as it is or cooked.

One way of cooking the *ika* is to cut along one side of the body pouch, so the whole pouch can be flattened out. Next, score diagonally at ¼-in/.5cm intervals, first one way then the other. This 'pine-cone' cutting has two functions. One is to stop the squid curling when it is cooked, and the other is to give an attractive texture. Cooking is very rapid; just drop the squid into a large pan of rapidly boiling water for only 15 seconds, then drain and cool.

Use this 'pine-cone' *ika* as the outer skin of a roll. Line the *ika* with *nori* (seaweed paper), then fill with sliced *shiitake* mushrooms and seasoned *kampyō* (pages 34 and 35), white fish meat, mange-touts (snow peas) and sushi rice. Roll in a *makisu*, then serve sliced.

Whole baby *ika* are sometimes cooked in a mixture of reduced *dashi* (stock/broth), soy sauce, *mirin* and sugar.

TEMAKI

A popular *temaki* at the Yamato is Salmon Skin Roll, made from a piece of salmon with the skin attached. It is grilled (broiled) from the skin side.

The grilled salmon is cut to strips.

A half sheet of nori is spread with a little rice, then the salmon is added with vegetables as shown.

Because the rice is not tight-packed – a typical roll contains little more rice than a piece of *nigiri-zushi* – *temaki* are less filling than other kinds of sushi, and are ideal for people who are watching their weight. They may even be rolled in things other than *nori*: lettuce, especially Cos (Romaine) lettuce, makes a light, refreshing roll.

Like a number of other things in this book, *temaki* are a relatively recent innovation in sushi. They are hand-rolled *maki* made without the aid of a *makisu* (rolling mat). Nevertheless, they have rapidly gained popularity. In some Japanese sushi bars, customers can order a *temaki* meal which consists of a box of rice, a box of *nori* (seaweed paper) and an assortment of sushi ingredients, including fish, *kampyō* (dried gourd) and pickles. The customers then make the rolls to their own taste.

You can do the same thing at home. *Temaki* lend themselves admirably to a sushi buffet, where your guests can help themselves to whatever they like. Any of the ingredients described in this book are suitable, but you might care to offer tuna, a bowl of hot-pepper marinade (page 85), prawns (shrimp), *kampyō*, cucumber and, of course, *gari* (pickled ginger) and *wasabi* (Japanese horse-radish).

Some people experiment with all kinds of other ingredients, such as cooked chicken, rare or raw beef, ham, cream cheese, *daikon* sprouts (white radish) and so forth. *Temaki* also offer a good way to experiment with ingredients you may not have tried before, such as *fuki* (boiled, salted coltsfoot, available in jars).

You can also use soft and semi-liquid ingredients such as roe or *uni* (sea urchin). In this case, it is easier to make the *temaki* slightly cone-shaped, with the rice at the bottom and the filling above it. Half-sheets of *nori* are easiest for this, though for buffets, quarter-sheets are arguably more manoeuverable and convivial, because people cluster around and make more of them!

The roll is somewhat conical, so the ingredients peep out of the wide end of the cone.

TIGER EYE

1 Slice through a fillet of raw squid to form a tube. Cutting like this, without cutting straight through at the sides, requires some skill!

Tiger Eye is one of the varieties of fancy sushi that *itamae* like to make to prove their virtuosity. It requires a fair amount of time, and some dexterity, to make.

2 On a half-sheet of *nori* (seaweed paper), place enough smoked salmon to cover about half the sheet. The salmon should go to the edge, but no further.

3 In the centre of th smoked salmon place a strip of *kam aboko* (white fis cake). Place a but ter-flied shrim (page 80) on top this.

4 Another layer smoked salmon com pletes this stage.

5 Roll up the *nori* wit the above ingredient and trim off an excess if the roll too big to fit into th slit in the squid.

6 Slide the *nori* roll into the slit in the squid.

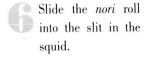

7 At this stage, the *nori* roll will be a loose fit. To shrink the squid around it, the whole thing is grilled (broiled) for a few minutes.

*The completed Tiger Eye is
sliced for serving.*

Katsuo *served as* nigiri-zushi.

TUNA (*Maguro*)
YELLOWTAIL (*Hamachi*)
BONITA (*Katsuo*)
AND
SWORDFISH (*Ma-kajiki*)

Maguro (tuna) and *hamachi* (yellowtail), a Pacific game fish related to tuna, are two of the classic sushi fish. Both are most often served in the same way, with bias-cut slices from fillets served as *nigiri-zushi* (finger sushi), though scraps of tuna are often used up in *maki* and both types of fish typically appear on a Rainbow Roll.

Both are big, fat fish, with the highest concentration of fat around the belly. Sushi made from either will vary considerably in taste and price, according to where it is cut from.

To illustrate this, the fattiest meat from a *maguro* is known as *ōtoro*; this is now the most prized cut of *maguro* (look for Toro Tuna on the menu) and is darker than the leaner orange meat; *chutoro*. The red meat around the spine is known as *akami*. The red meat from the strong tail muscles is the cheapest cut but is still delicious. Like *hamachi*, *maguro* is filleted as *gomai-oroshi* (five-piece cut), with each of the side fillets cut lengthwise into two blocks or *cho*.

Hamachi are somewhat smaller, and there is less variation in the meat than with tuna. *Hamachi* sushi from the upper *cho* is normally cut so there is a band or corner of dark meat *(chiai)* at the end of the slice of meat; to lovers of strong sushi, this is delicious, but some people find it too fishy. Sushi from the lower *cho* does not always have this.

Katsuo (bonita), a variety of tuna popular in California, with its dark red flesh, is even smaller than *hamachi* and displays still less variation in flavour from cut to cut. Sometimes, *katsuo* is lightly grilled on a skewer over an open flame, then cooled rapidly in ice water before being sliced for sushi or sashimi.

Ma-kajiki (swordfish) was once the most highly prized of all fish for sushi, but it has somewhat fallen from favour. As with *hamachi*, some people find *ma-kajiki* too fishy-tasting. Besides, good, fresh *ma-kajiki* are hard to get. These great 6ft/2m fish are prepared in the same way as *maguro* or *hamachi*. The flesh, which is white when cooked, has a brownish tinge when raw and looks somewhat like discoloured tuna.

When grilling katsuo *over an open flame, bamboo skewers may burn at the ends, but they will greatly reduce the risk of burning your fingers!*

Maguro *served as* nigiri-zushi.

THE FOUR SEASONS

The Japanese are acutely aware of the seasons. One of the classical requirements of the *haiku*, the Japanese 17-syllable verse form, is that it contains a reference to the season for which it was written.

The only trouble is that in a world that is linked by air-freighted sushi, season no longer has the impact that it once did. Even the time-honoured advice to avoid oysters when there isn't an 'R' in the month (May, June, July, August) is no longer valid when they are so widely farmed.

Also, freezing makes a big difference. If oily fish is frozen within a few hours, or even minutes, of being caught, as can happen on some of the big, modern factory ships, it can successfully be thawed and even used for sushi. With yellowtail (which is commercially farmed in Japan), it is hard to tell the difference from fresh fish. Lean fish, on the other hand, can suffer badly from freezing.

What is more, various types of fish may be *available* all year around, but the price in winter (when the fishermen are less willing to go to sea!) can be twice as high as in the summer. Ordinary *chutoro* tuna can easily cost two, three or even four times as much as fillet steak (*filet mignon*).

To top it all, different kinds of the same fish may be in season at different times of year. For example, the Meiji Tuna is reckoned to be at its best in summer, while the Boston Tuna is an autumn fish; and while sea urchins from California are at their best in summer and autumn, sea urchins from Maine are most desirable in winter and spring. If a fishmonger cares enough about his wares to label (or even to know) their provenance, he also knows enough to advise you on what is best.

Because a book like this is designed to sell throughout the world, a meaningful guide to the seasons is impossible; everything depends on local conditions. The best way to find out about the seasons is experience – some types of fish will taste better at some times of year than others. If you cultivate the acquaintance of a reliable fishmonger as well, and eat at a good sushi bar where the *itamae* will tell you what is best, it will take you about a year to learn all about the seasons in your part of the world.

As a *very* general guide, though, most fish in cold waters are at their best in the autumn, as they fatten up for the winter; warm-water fish are at their best in spring and summer, when food is plentiful and they grow large and strong; and in the winter, the best bets are mostly the oily fleshed fish such as mackerel and herring. Flatfish are often good in the spring.

Among shellfish, summer is a surprisingly good season for many species. The old injunctions against eating them at this time of year were more to do with the risk of spoilage than with any defects in flavour. Octopus and squid are good in winter and spring, though, and prawns (shrimp) and many clams are good in winter.

The widest choice is usually in the spring, closely followed by summer. The smallest choice is in winter, with the autumn as an intermediate season.

JAPANESE-ENGLISH
GLOSSARY

*G*E
ep-fried tofu

*K*AGAI
k shell

*K*AMI
rk meat from the centre of a fish
ge 92)

*N*AGO
nger or sea eel

O-NORI
ked seaweed

*O*YAGI
und clam

*W*ABI
alone

*K*AGAI
Aoyagi

*N*CHA
e of tea

*U*RI
lowtail

*I*A

*I*AI
k outer meat (page 92)

*I*IRASHI-ZUSHI
ttered sushi

*I*UTORO
ty tuna (page 92)

*I*IKON
anese radish

*S*HI
h stock

*I*I
wn (shrimp) or lobster

*I*GAWA
at next to the fins on a flatfish
ge 30)

*K*I
sfoot (page 88)

*G*U
w-fish

TO-MAKI
ge roll

*R*I
kled ginger

GOMA
Sesame seed

GOMAI OROSHI
Five-fillet cut for fish (page 30)

GOMOKU-ZUSHI
Mixed scattered sushi

GUNKAN-MAKI
'Battleship' sushi

GYOKURO
Superior green tea

HAKO-ZUSHI
Box or pressed sushi

HAMACHI
A young yellowtail

HANGIRI
Rice tub

HASHIRA
Part of shellfish (page 52)

HIKARI-MONO
'Things that shine' (page 62)

HIMO
Part of shellfish (page 52)

HIRAME
Halibut

HIYASHI-WAKAME
see *Wakame*

HŌCHŌ
Knives

HOSO-MAKI
Small rolls

HOTATE-GAI
Scallops

IKA Squid

IKURA
Salmon roe

INARI-ZUSHI
Stuffed deep-fried bean curd

ITAMAE
Sushi chef

KAKI
Oysters

KAMABOKO
Fish cake

KANI
Crab

KAMPYŌ
Dried gourd

KAPPA
Cucumber

KATSUO
Bonita

KATSUO-BUSHI
Dried bonita flakes

KAZU-NO-KO
Herring roe

KISU
Sillago

KOHADA
Gizzard shad

KOMBU
Type of seaweed

KONOSHIRO
A gizzard shad

MAGURO
Blue fin tuna

MA-KAJIKI
Swordfish

MAKI
Rolled sushi

MAKISU
Bamboo rolling mat

MIRIN
Sweet cooking *sake*

MIRU-GAI
Horse-clam, geoduck

MISO
Fermented soya bean paste

MISO-DASHI
Type of soup

MOMIGI-OROSHI
Hot-pepper paste

MUSHI-ZUSHI
Steamed sushi

NAKA-ZUMI
see *Kohada*

NARE-ZUSHI
Fermented sushi

NATTŌ
Glutinous soya beans

NIGIRI-ZUSHI
Squeezed or pressed sushi

NINJIN
Carrot

NORI
Seaweed paper

OBORO
Sweetened fish product (page 56)

ŌTORO
Fatty cut of tuna

PONZU
Citrus vinegar (page 58)

SABA
Mackerel

SAKE
Rice wine

SAKE
Salmon (pronounced differently from *sake*)

SAKUDORI
Way of cutting fish (page 24)

SANMAI OROSHI
Three-fillet cut for fish (page 28)

SASHIMI
Raw fish, served without rice

SAYORI
Halfbeak

SENCHA
A middle grade green tea

SHAMOJI
Rice paddle

SHIITAKE
Type of mushroom, usually dried

SHINKO
see *Kohada*

SHISO
Beefsteak plant

SHŌYU
Soy sauce

SU Rice vinegar

SUDARE
Another name for *makisu*

SUDORI SHOGA
Another name for *gari* (pickled ginger)

SUIMONO
Type of soup

SUSHI-ZU
Spiced, sweetened vinegar (page 42)

SUZUKI
Sea bass

SUZUKO
see *Ikura*

TAI
Sea bream

TAKO
Octopus

TAMAGO
Egg

TARAKO
Cod roe

TEMAKI
Hand-rolled sushi

TŌFU
Bean curd

TORI-GAI
Cockle

TSU
Knowledgeable sushi lover

TSU-ME
Thick brushing sauce (page 76)

UCHIWA
A fan

UME-BOSHI
Pickled plums

UNAGI
Freshwater eel

UNI
Sea urchin

WAKAME
Type of seaweed (page 40)

WAKEGI
Spring onions, green onions, scallions

WASABI
Japanese horseradish or
Japanese mustard

YUNOMI
Large tea cup

ZARU
Bamboo drainer

INDEX